WILLA CATHER

Writing about the American Frontier

Tammy Orr Staats

Boston, Massachusetts
Chandler, Arizona
Glenview, Illinois
Upper Saddle River, New Jersey

Illustrations
Opener, 1, 8, 9, 10, 12, 15 Mike Lacey; 7 Joe LeMonnier.

Photographs
Every effort has been made to secure permission and provide appropriate credit for photographic material. The publisher deeply regrets any omission and pledges to correct errors called to its attention in subsequent editions.

Unless otherwise acknowledged, all photographs are the property of Pearson Education, Inc.

Photo locators denoted as follows: Top (T), Center (C), Bottom (B), Left (L), Right (R), Background (Bkgd)

Opener: (Bkgrd) Prints & Photographs Division, LC-DIG-ppmsca-08375/Library of Congress; 2 Prints & Photographs Division, LC-USZ62-82912/Library of Congress; 3 An American Time Capsule, Rare Book and Special Collections Division, rbpe13401300/Library of Congress; 4 Jupiterimages/Thinkstock; 5 Prints & Photographs Division, LC-DIG-ppmsca-08378/Library of Congress; 6 FSA/OWI Collection, Prints & Photographs Division, LC-USF34-008666-D/Library of Congress; 11 Prints & Photographs Division, LC-DIG-ppmsca-08375 /Library of Congress; 13 FSA/OWI Collection, Prints & Photographs Division, LC-USF33-001468-M3/Library of Congress.

Copyright © 2013 by Pearson Education, Inc., or its affiliates. All rights reserved. Printed in the United States of America. This publication is protected by copyright, and permission should be obtained from the publisher prior to any prohibited reproduction, storage in a retrieval system, or transmission in any form by any means, electronic, mechanical, photocopying, recording, or likewise. For information regarding permissions, write to Pearson Curriculum Rights & Permissions, One Lake Street, Upper Saddle River, New Jersey 07458.

Pearson® is a trademark, in the U.S. and/or in other countries, of Pearson Inc. or its affiliates.

ISBN-13: 978-0-328-67646-0
ISBN-10:   0-328-67646-2

6 7 8 9 V0FL 17 16 15 14

A Famous Writer

Willa Cather's life was an adventure. In 1883, her family left the woods and mountains of Virginia to begin a new life in the Midwest. They were **pioneers** who made the move along with thousands of other families.

The Nebraska **prairie** where the Cather family settled was unlike any place that Willa Cather had ever seen before. Gone were the mountains and thick woods of Virginia. Instead, she saw a flat landscape with tall grasses stretching as far as she could see.

While there were few roads and towns, there *were* neighbors. Many were **immigrants** from different countries. They had come west to the **frontier** with the hope of a fresh start and a new life.

Later Cather became famous writing about people very much like those she had met in her childhood. Today, Willa Cather is considered one of America's great writers. She is remembered for her lively portraits of immigrants and pioneers on the prairie.

Early Years

The oldest of seven children, Willa Cather was born in Virginia on December 7, 1873. The family lived in the beautiful Shenandoah Valley, in a home called Willow Shade.

Cather's uncle had recently moved to a **homestead** in the plains of Nebraska. Many others were also moving west. They had read ads and pamphlets that promised a wonderful life and a plot of land. Farming the land, they were told, would be easy.

This sounded appealing to Cather's father. A number of Cather's relatives had died of tuberculosis. This is a disease that most frequently attacks the lungs, the part of the body that controls breathing. It was said that the prairie offered a good climate for weak lungs.

An advertisement for land

The Big Move

In 1883, a fire destroyed the sheep barn at Willow Shade. The Cather family decided it was the time to move. In the spring of 1883, nine-year-old Willa Cather, her parents, three siblings, her grandmother, and several other family members made their way across the country by train. When they arrived at the train station in Red Cloud, Nebraska, a wagon and team of horses took them the sixteen miles to their destination.

Cather was startled by what she saw. Instead of the rolling hills and mountains of Virginia, she saw nothing but a flat, treeless landscape. She felt as if she "had been jerked away from all of these things and thrown into a country as bare as a piece of sheet iron." She said: "As we drove further and further into the country, I felt . . . as if we had come to the end of everything."

The Nebraska prairie

A house made of grass-covered dirt called sod

A New Life

At first, Cather felt lonely and homesick. The life of a homesteader was not an easy one. While the Cathers lived in a simple wood-framed house, many homesteaders lived in simpler houses made of blocks of **sod**. And because many settlers had never farmed before, many farms failed.

Despite all this, Cather found herself beginning to appreciate the vast open spaces that surrounded her. She once said that trees were so rare in this area that people visited them as if they were people. In spite of the lack of trees, Cather was falling in love with the Nebraska prairie.

A one-room schoolhouse

In Virginia, Cather probably didn't hear many people speak a language other than English. But in Nebraska, there were immigrants from many countries who spoke many different languages. Cather attended school in a one-room schoolhouse, but her most valuable education came from spending time with the many immigrants she met. She came to appreciate and respect their **cultures** and the lives they had left behind.

A Second Move

Less than a year after their arrival in Nebraska, Cather's father decided to quit farming. He moved his family to the town of Red Cloud, where he became a businessman.

Life in this town of 2,000 people was far different from life on the farm, 16 miles away. Cather enjoyed her new life. There was a little opera house in Red Cloud, and Cather fell in love with the music and shows she saw there. She met an Englishman who offered to teach her to read Greek and Latin. A Jewish family that had recently come from Europe allowed Cather to borrow from their large collection of books.

The Cather Family Homes

A Strong Personality

At the age of 11, Cather got a job delivering mail. Every day she rode from farm to farm bringing letters and packages. Cather would stop and chat along the way. The older immigrant women especially fascinated Cather. She spent hours chatting with them. Later, Cather said, "I particularly liked the old women; they understood my homesickness and were kind to me."

At the age of 15, Cather decided she wanted to be a surgeon. However, in the 1880s, many did not think this an appropriate career for a woman. In fact, there were only a few hundred female doctors in the entire country. Cather was, however, determined. For a time, she cut her hair short, dressed like a man and called herself Wm. Cather, M.D. *Wm.* is an abbreviation for the name "William." She joined local doctors on their visits to care for the sick.

The Cather's home in Red Cloud, Nebraska

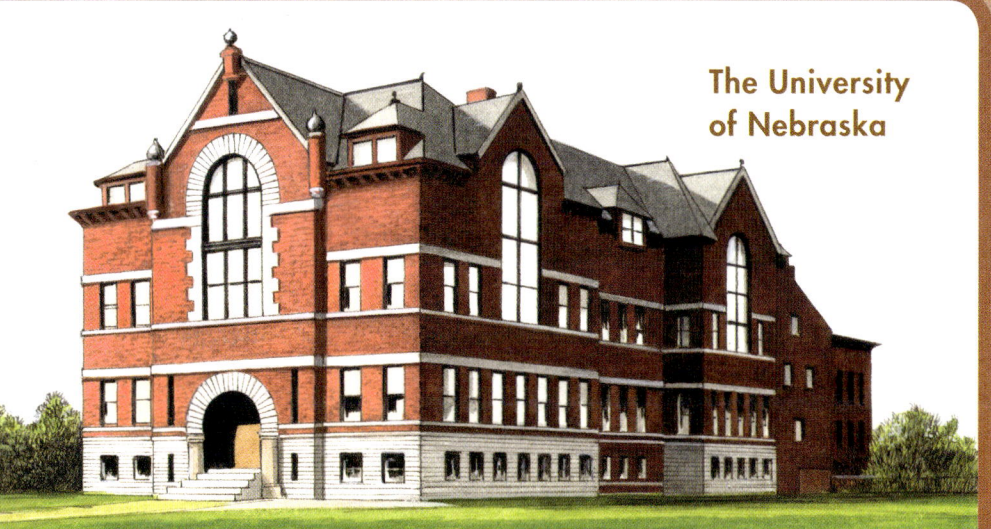

The University of Nebraska

Becoming a Writer

When Cather graduated from the one-room schoolhouse in 1890, she was one of only three members of her class. She proudly gave the graduation speech. Then, at the age of 16, Cather left for the University of Nebraska in Lincoln. She intended to study science there. She had not given up the dream of becoming a doctor.

Then something happened which changed her plans. Without Cather's knowledge, an English professor submitted one of her **essays** to a newspaper. Cather was shocked and thrilled when she learned her writing had been published. Seeing her name in print made her revise her career plans. Now, she realized that she wanted to become a writer. She was just as determined to succeed as ever.

    After graduating from college, Cather lived in Red Cloud. Later she moved to Pennsylvania. For over a decade, Cather made her living writing and editing for newspapers and magazines. She also taught high school. Cather's first published book was a collection of her poems.

    However, by 1911, Cather's focus had turned to writing **novels**. And, in time, she began to write about what she knew—the prairie and its people.

    Cather once said that the most important years in a writer's life were those between the ages of eight and fifteen. These were the years in which people soaked up the world around them. For Cather these were the years spent in Nebraska. Cather's stories began to focus on the life and pioneer spirit of immigrants. Cather made this feel real. She had, after all, seen it all firsthand.

O Pioneers!

Cather's second novel was a great success. *O Pioneers!* tells the story of Alexandra Bergman, the daughter of an immigrant who comes to Nebraska. He tries to farm but fails at it. Just before his death, he makes a request. He asks his daughter, not his two sons, to take over the farm.

Cather's father had once said to her, "You have to show grit in a new country." Cather's character, Alexandra, has *grit*, another word for strength or courage. Alexandra has the tough spirit of the pioneers.

A pioneer family

My Ántonia

   Many people consider Cather's fourth novel to be her best. In *My Ántonia*, Cather tells the story of an immigrant family. The father, who was a violinist in Europe, left behind a culture he loves. He finds himself living in a sod house in the middle of the prairie. His family does not know the first thing about farming. He insists on dressing up every day in clothes that he wore in the "old country." Cather's novel shows how difficult it was for many immigrants to adapt to a new culture.

My Ántonia was published in 1918.

Cather based her characters on the people she met in the Midwest.

Cather's Writing

Willa Cather's characters, like Cather herself, have a powerful connection to the land on which they live. Cather wrote about this. "There was nothing but land; not a country at all, but the material of which countries are made."

Cather's writing was unusual for the time. Her stories were moving, but the language was plain. It was straightforward, just like the lives of her characters. When talking about the characters in a book, she once said, "You have then to give voice to the hearts of men . . . you can do it only so far as you have known them, loved them."

Her ability to tell the story of these pioneers was Cather's great gift to her readers. With the publication of each new book, Cather became more respected and well known as a writer. In 1922, Cather won the Pulitzer Prize, which is one of the most important prizes in America for writers. She won this award for her fifth novel, *One of Ours*.

A Long Career

Throughout her life, Cather continued to return from time to time to Red Cloud. She always took the time to visit her old friends. She would send them gifts during the holidays. During hard times, she sent them money and clothes.

Willa Cather had a long and successful career as a writer. She wrote essays, poems, short stories, and twelve novels. She also traveled around the country giving lectures and became friends with many highly respected writers.

Timeline of Willa Cather's Life

1873 Cather is born in Virginia.

1884 Cather's family moves to the town of Red Cloud.

1913 Cather publishes *O Pioneers!*

1870 — 1880 — 1890 — 1900

1883 Cather's family moves to a farm in Nebraska.

1891 Cather begins to attend University of Nebraska.

Willa Cather died on April 24, 1947, in the New York City apartment that had become her home. She was buried in Jaffrey, New Hampshire, near the mountains she had come to love later in life. As a famous writer, she had visited many places. Regardless of where she traveled, she never forgot the vast, grassy prairie that had been her childhood home.

1922
Cather wins the Pulitzer Prize.

1920   1930   1940   1950

1918
Cather publishes *My Antonia*.

1947
Cather dies in New York City.

Glossary

culture the way of life of a group of people

custom a way of doing something that has been handed down over time

essay a short piece of nonfiction writing on a specific topic

frontier the edge of a settled area

homestead farmland given free by the government to pioneers who were willing to settle a specific area

immigrant a person who moves to a new country

novel a long fictional story by a writer

pioneer someone who is among the first people to settle in an area

prairie a large, mostly flat, area of grassland without trees

sod soil covered with thick grass